The Music of Jerome Kern for S

Jerome Kern Saxophone.

Wise Publications
London/New York/Sydney

Exclusive Distributors:
Music Sales Limited
8/9 Frith Street, London W1V 5TZ, England.
Music Sales Pty Limited
120 Rothschild Avenue, Rosebery, NSW 2018, Australia.

This book © Copyright 1990 by Wise Publications
Order No. AM80524
UK ISBN 0.7119.2351.5

Designed by Pearce Marchbank Studio
Arranged by Robin De Smet
Music processed by MSS Studios

Music Sales' complete catalogue lists thousands of titles and is free from your local music shop, or direct from Music Sales Limited. Please send £1.75 in stamps for postage to Music Sales Limited, 8/9 Frith Street, London W1V 5TZ.

Unauthorised reproduction of any part of this publication by any means including photocopying is an infringement of copyright.

Printed in the United Kingdom by
J.B. Offset Printers (Marks Tey) Limited, Marks Tey, Essex.

A Fine Romance 4
All The Things You Are 6
All Through The Day 8
Bill 10
Can't Help Lovin' Dat Man 12
Dearly Beloved 16
I Dream Too Much 14
I'm Old Fashioned 18
I've Told Ev'ry Little Star 20
Long Ago And Far Away 17
Look For The Silver Lining 22
Make Believe 24
Ol' Man River 26
Pick Yourself Up 28
She Didn't Say 'Yes' 30
Smoke Gets In Your Eyes 31
The Folks Who Live On The Hill 32
The Last Time I Saw Paris 34
The Song Is You 46
The Touch Of Your Hand 36
The Way You Look Tonight 38
They Didn't Believe Me 40
Who 42
Why Do I Love You 44
Yesterdays 47

A Fine Romance

Music by Jerome Kern. Words by Dorothy Fields

© Copyright 1936 T.B. Harms & Company Incorporated, USA.
Chappell Music Limited, 129 Park Street, London W1/Polygram Music Publishing Limited, 30 Berkeley Square, London W1.
All Rights Reserved. International Copyright Secured.

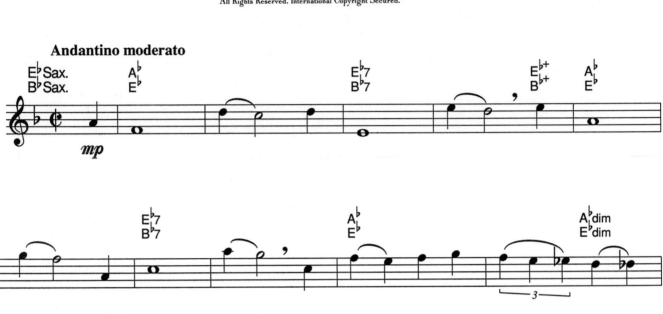

All The Things You Are
Music by Jerome Kern. Words by Oscar Hammerstein II

© Copyright 1939 T.B. Harms & Company Incorporated, USA.
Polygram Music Publishing Limited, 30 Berkeley Square, London W1.
All Rights Reserved. International Copyright Secured.

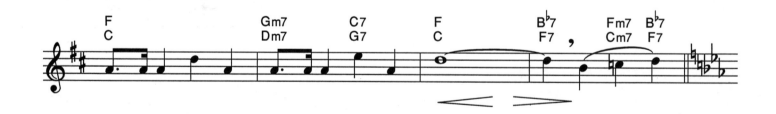

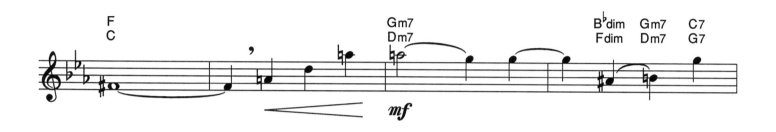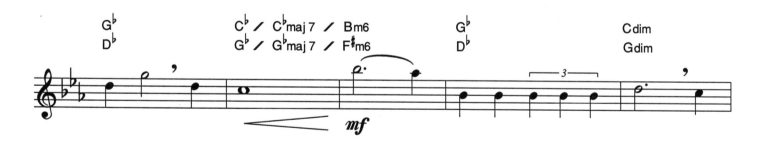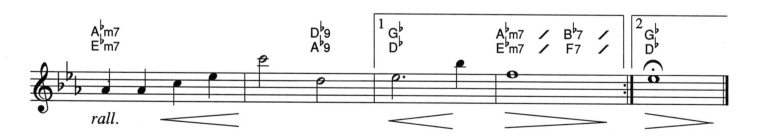

All Through The Day
Music by Jerome Kern. Words by Oscar Hammerstein II

© Copyright 1946 T.B. Harms & Company Incorporated, USA.
Polygram Music Publishing Limited, 30 Berkeley Square, London W1.
All Rights Reserved. International Copyright Secured.

Can't Help Lovin' Dat Man

Music by Jerome Kern. Words by Oscar Hammerstein II

© Copyright 1927 T.B. Harms & Company Incorporated, USA.
Polygram Music Publishing Limited, 30 Berkeley Square, London W1.
All Rights Reserved. International Copyright Secured.

I Dream Too Much

Music by Jerome Kern. Words by Otto Harbach

© Copyright 1935 T.B. Harms & Company Incorporated, USA.
Polygram Music Publishing Limited, 30 Berkeley Square, London W1 (50%)/Chappell Music Limited, 129 Park Street, London W1 (50%).
All Rights Reserved. International Copyright Secured.

Dearly Beloved

Music by Jerome Kern. Words by Johnny Mercer

© Copyright 1942 T.B. Harms & Company Incorporated, USA.
Polygram Music Publishing Limited, 30 Berkeley Square, London W1/Chappell Music Limited, 129 Park Street, London W1.
All Rights Reserved. International Copyright Secured.

Long Ago And Far Away

Music by Jerome Kern. Words by Ira Gershwin

© Copyright 1944 T.B. Harms & Company Incorporated, USA.
Polygram Music Publishing Limited, 30 Berkeley Square, London W1/Chappell Music Limited, 129 Park Street, London W1.
All Rights Reserved. International Copyright Secured.

I'm Old Fashioned

Music by Jerome Kern. Words by Johnny Mercer

© Copyright 1942 T.B. Harms & Company Incorporated, USA.
Polygram Music Publishing Limited, 30 Berkeley Square, London W1/Chappell Music Limited, 129 Park Street, London W1.
All Rights Reserved. International Copyright Secured.

Moderately

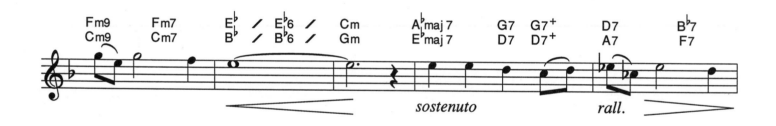

I've Told Ev'ry Little Star

Music by Jerome Kern. Words by Oscar Hammerstein II

© Copyright 1932 T.B. Harms & Company Incorporated, USA.
Polygram Music Publishing Limited, 30 Berkeley Square, London W1.
All Rights Reserved. International Copyright Secured.

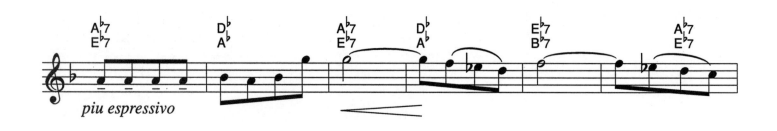

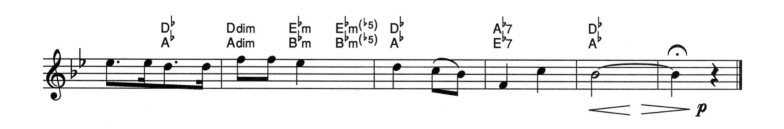

Look For The Silver Lining

Music by Jerome Kern. Words by Buddy De Sylva

© Copyright 1920 T.B. Harms & Company Incorporated, USA.
Polygram Music Publishing Limited, 30 Berkeley Square, London W1.
Redwood Music Limited, 14 New Burlington Street, London W1.
All Rights Reserved. International Copyright Secured.

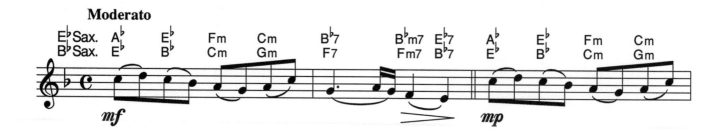

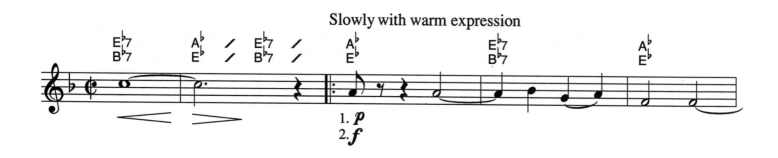

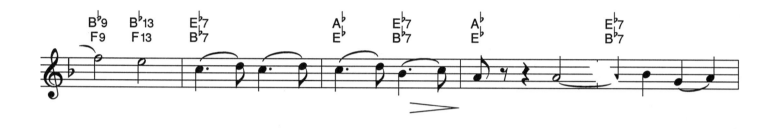

Make Believe

Music by Jerome Kern. Words by Oscar Hammerstein II

© Copyright 1927 T.B. Harms & Company Incorporated, USA.
Polygram Music Publishing Limited, 30 Berkeley Square, London W1.
All Rights Reserved. International Copyright Secured.

Ol' Man River

Music by Jerome Kern. Words by Oscar Hammerstein II

© Copyright 1927 T.B. Harms & Company Incorporated, USA.
Polygram Music Publishing Limited, 30 Berkeley Square, London W1.
All Rights Reserved. International Copyright Secured.

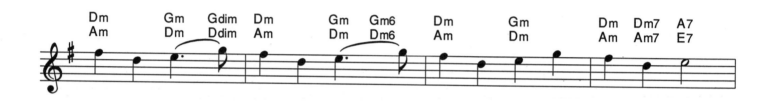

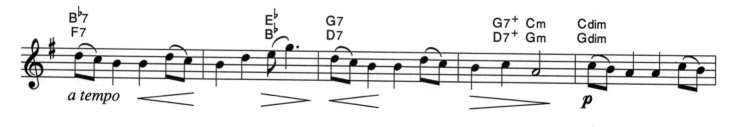

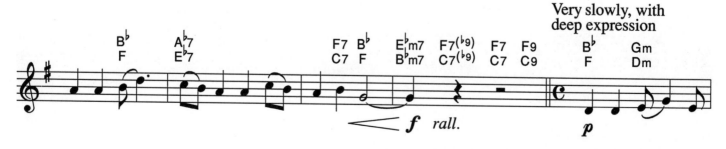

Pick Yourself Up

Music by Jerome Kern. Words by Dorothy Fields

© Copyright 1936 T.B. Harms & Company Incorporated, USA.
Chappell Music Limited, 129 Park Street, London W1/Polygram Music Publishing Limited, 30 Berkeley Square, London W1.
All Rights Reserved. International Copyright Secured.

She Didn't Say 'Yes'

Music by Jerome Kern. Words by Otto Harbach

© Copyright 1931 T.B. Harms & Company Incorporated, USA.
Redwood Music Limited, Iron Bridge House, 3 Bridge Approach, London NW1 (50%)/Polygram Music Publishing Limited,
30 Berkeley Square, London W1 (50%).
All Rights Reserved. International Copyright Secured.

Smoke Gets In Your Eyes

Music by Jerome Kern. Words by Otto Harbach

© Copyright 1934 T.B. Harms & Company Incorporated, USA.
Redwood Music Limited, Iron Bridge House, 3 Bridge Approach, London NW1/Polygram Music Publishing Limited, 30 Berkeley Square, London W1.
All Rights Reserved. International Copyright Secured.

The Folks Who Live On The Hill

Music by Jerome Kern. Words by Oscar Hammerstein II

© Copyright 1937 T.B. Harms & Company Incorporated, USA.
Polygram Music Publishing Limited, 30 Berkeley Square, London W1.
All Rights Reserved. International Copyright Secured.

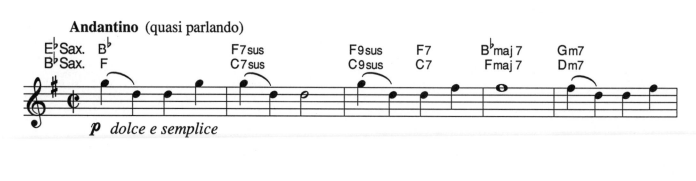

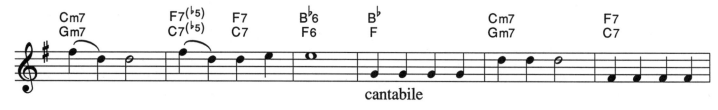

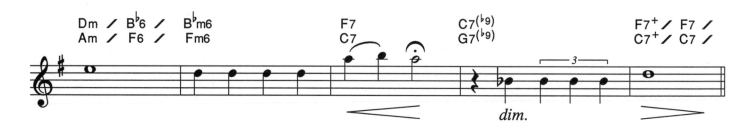

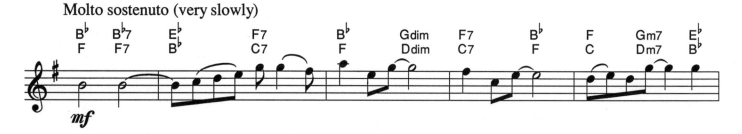

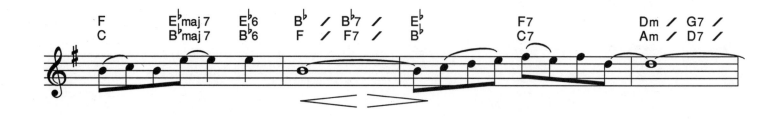

The Last Time I Saw Paris

Music by Jerome Kern. Words by Oscar Hammerstein II

© Copyright 1940 T.B. Harms & Company Incorporated, USA.
Polygram Music Publishing Limited, 30 Berkeley Square, London W1.
All Rights Reserved. International Copyright Secured.

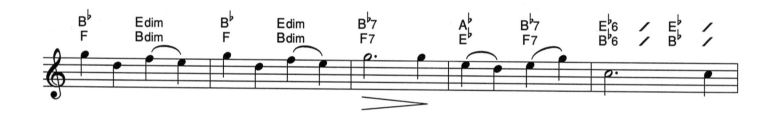

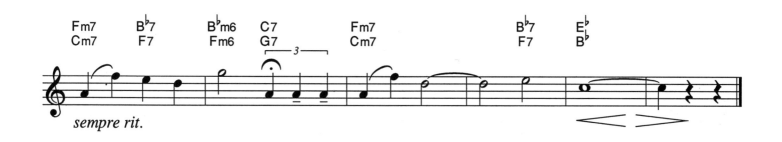

The Touch Of Your Hand

Music by Jerome Kern. Words by Otto Harbach

© Copyright 1933 T.B. Harms & Company Incorporated, USA.
Redwood Music Limited, Iron Bridge House, 3 Bridge Approach, London NW1/Polygram Music Publishing Limited, 30 Berkeley Square, London W1.
All Rights Reserved. International Copyright Secured.

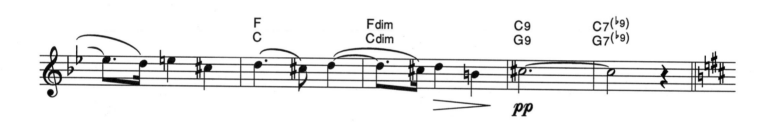
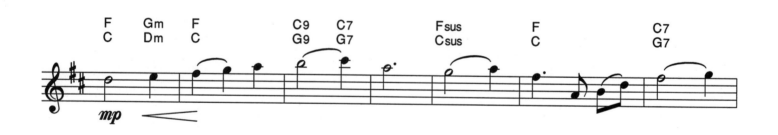

They Didn't Believe Me

Music by Jerome Kern. Words by Herbert Reynolds

© Copyright 1914 T.B. Harms & Company Incorporated, USA.
Francis, Day & Hunter Limited, London WC2/Polygram Music Publishing Limited, 30 Berkeley Square, London W1
All Rights Reserved. International Copyright Secured.

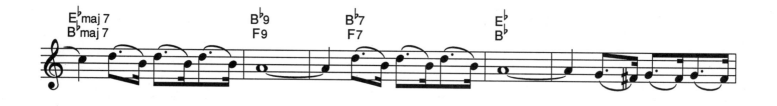

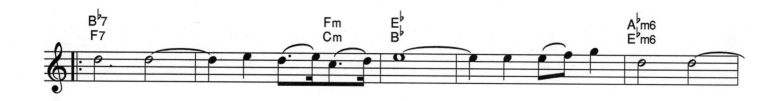

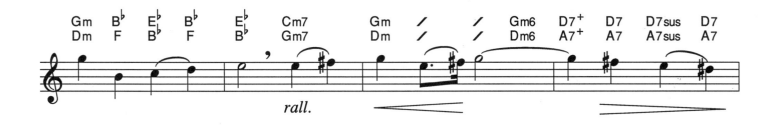

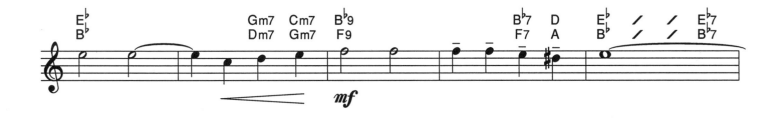

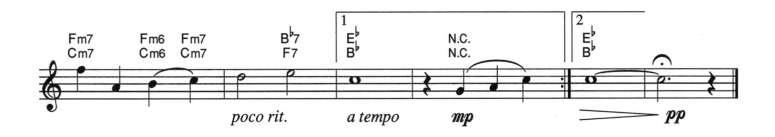

Who

Music by Jerome Kern. Words by Otto Harbach & Oscar Hammerstein II

© Copyright 1925 T.B. Harms & Company Incorporated, USA.
Polygram Music Publishing Limited, 30 Berkeley Square, London W1 (75%)/Redwood Music Limited, Iron Bridge House, 3 Bridge Approach, London NW1 (25%)
All Rights Reserved. International Copyright Secured.

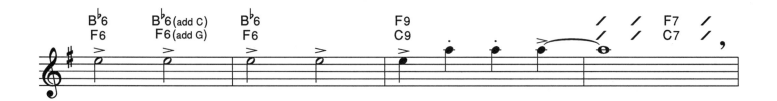

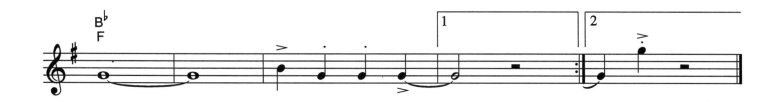

Why Do I Love You

Music by Jerome Kern. Words by Oscar Hammerstein II

© Copyright 1927 T.B. Harms & Company Incorporated, USA.
Polygram Music Publishing Limited, 30 Berkeley Square, London W1.
All Rights Reserved. International Copyright Secured.

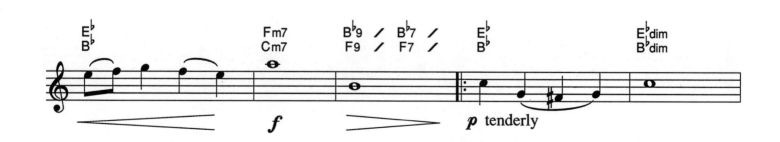

The Song Is You

Music by Jerome Kern. Words by Oscar Hammerstein II

© Copyright 1932 T.B. Harms & Company Incorporated, USA.
Polygram Music Publishing Limited, 30 Berkeley Square, London W1.
All Rights Reserved. International Copyright Secured.

Yesterdays

Music by Jerome Kern. Words by Otto Harbach

© Copyright 1933 T.B. Harms & Company Incorporated, USA.
Redwood Music Limited, Iron Bridge House, 3 Bridge Approach, London NW1/Polygram Music Publishing Limited, 30 Berkeley Square, London W1.
All Rights Reserved. International Copyright Secured.